Appliqué
Masterpiece
SERIES

Hearts & Tulips

D1611583

Margaret Docherty

American Quilter's Society
P. O. Box 3290 • Paducah, KY 42002-3290
www.AmericanQuilter.com

Located in Paducah, Kentucky, the American Quilter's Society (AQS) is dedicated to promoting the accomplishments of today's quilters. Through its publications and events, AQS strives to honor today's quiltmakers and their work and to inspire future creativity and innovation in quiltmaking.

SENIOR EDITOR: LINDA BAXTER LASCO
GRAPHIC DESIGN: ELAINE WILSON
COVER DESIGN: MICHAEL BUCKINGHAM
PHOTOGRAPHY: CHARLES R. LYNCH, UNLESS OTHERWISE NOTED

Additional copies of this book may be ordered from the American Quilter's Society, PO Box 3290, Paducah, KY 42002-3290, or online at www.AmericanQuilter.com.

Text © 2008, Author, Margaret Docherty
Artwork © 2008, American Quilter's Society

Library of Congress Cataloging-in-Publication Data

Docherty, Margaret.
  Appliqué masterpiece series. Hearts and tulips / by Margaret Docherty.
    p. cm.
  ISBN 978-1-57432-974-2
  1. Appliqué--Patterns. 2. Quilting--Patterns. 3. Quilts. I. Title.

TT779.D634 2009
746.44'5046--dc22
                   2008049683

American Quilter's Society
P. O. Box 3290 • Paducah, KY 42002-3290
www.AmericanQuilter.com

Proudly printed and bound in the United States of America

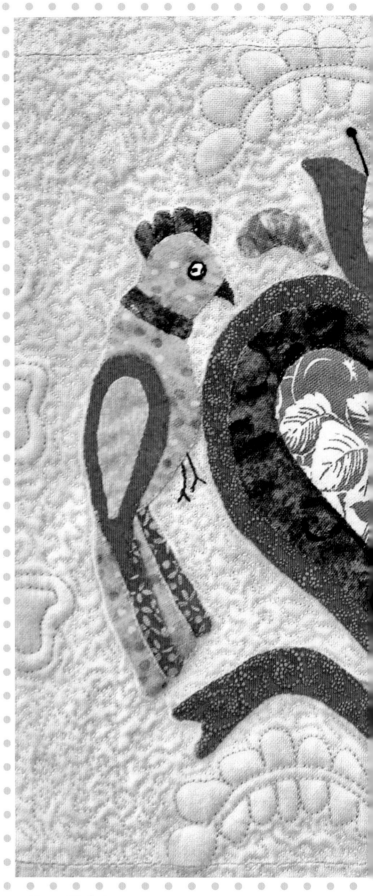

PHOTO: Margaret Docherty

Dedication

For my family, who always praise my work, perhaps sometimes unwisely, cook for me, photograph quilting things endlessly, fix computer problems, and even help with the ironing when I am writing a book or finishing a quilt.

To Brian, Jenny, Mary, and Alexis, thank you all so very much.

PHOTO: Margaret Docherty

Acknowledgments

Alexander Long for his photography.

The many historians with an interest in the first American settlers who
have kindly put their knowledge and opinions in the public domain.

Contents

Preface

In the 21st century most people associate the tulip with The Netherlands (Holland). A visit there in early spring is an unforgettable sight with field upon field of colorful tulips of all shapes and sizes in full bloom, an inspiration for any quilter.

The Dutch are renowned worldwide for their ability to cultivate; they export a huge variety of bulbs, ornamental plants, and cut flowers as well as fruit and vegetables. However, they are best known for their tulips.

It is ironic that the tulip is not a naturally occurring flower of The Netherlands. It is said that the nearest "wild" tulip is 500 miles away. Tulips were probably imported to The Netherlands from Turkey, Asia, and Russia. Their Eastern origins may account for the name *tulip*. The flower resembles a turban, *tulipa* being the modern Latin name for this Eastern headwear.

The first tulips arrived in The Netherlands in 1593 and for the next 44 years their market value was astounding. Many made a fortune dealing in tulip bulbs. There was no limit to the price the rich would pay for an exciting new bulb. However, rather like the Wall Street Crash of 1929, the bottom fell out of the tulip trade in 1637. Although no longer a valuable commodity, the tulip has remained an emblem and major export of The Netherlands, and Tulip Fever, or Tulipomania, has remained a well-documented piece of history.

Tulipomania, however, focussed on the real thing. My ideas for the tulip designs in this book came from a different source, although geographically originating just next door to The Netherlands. Tulips and hearts appeared in the folk art of many European countries, such as Hungary, long before tulipomania hit "Holland."

The early German-speaking immigrants arriving in America settled in Pennsylvania, and as time passed they became known to their English speaking neighbors as "Pennsylvania Dutch," from the German "Deutsch."

These early settlers brought with them and further developed an art form that is now recognized worldwide and is popularly, but not accurately, known as Pennsylvania "Dutch" Folk Art.

Flowers, hearts, birds, and angels appear in beautiful *fraktur* documents. These designs have also been embroidered, woven into tapestries, and stitched into quilts. Furniture, such as wedding chests, have been lovingly painted with hearts and flowers and, famously, barn doors have acquired a very specific folk art design, the *hex*.

The early German-speaking settlers left their homeland often because of religious persecution and poverty. Despite their past hardships and the difficulties of settling into a new country, they remembered their native arts and today we must be grateful that such a rich tapestry of folk art has been preserved for us all to enjoy.

The tulip has a history of undoubted complexity and fascination. Fortunes have been won and lost trading bulbs and it is a symbol of European culture from beyond the Middle Ages.

Back home, here in England, we have the rose, and in the name of the rose the realm itself was at stake. But roses are more difficult to appliqué, so another quilt, another book, another time.

PHOTO: Margaret Docherty

PHOTO: Margaret Docherty

Hearts & Tulips ✢ Margaret Docherty

Introduction

Those who appreciate fine art will describe folk art as primitive, its roots embedded in rural or unsophisticated societies and showing a notable lack of perspective and proportion. For the needle-woman, colorful designs with simple lines translate well into fabric or embroidery and folk art has long been a favorite source of patterns for her.

Of all the folk art motifs, the most enduring and endearing by far has been the tulip. Combined with a heart, many possibilities for design arise.

I searched for some time to explain the many tulips in Pennsylvania Dutch folk art, but now believe there is no more complicated a reason than the flower is easy to draw. Three petals, and you are there. Anyone can manage to draw a tulip and those without fine art skills can still indulge their love of design and color.

The blocks in this book are my own design and I cannot claim that they are an updated representation of original folk art designs, but they are near enough in style. However, you will find many of the original concepts of Pennsylvania Dutch folk art motifs in the patterns. The tulips come in all shapes and sizes and are accompanied by hearts, doves, parrots, and colorful small birds.

Many of the original folk art designs were worked in embroidery stitches and the motifs were complex—too complex for a small quilt block. What I aimed to create was an impression of the folk art of yesterday in appliqué using simple patterns.

The 36 blocks of the quilt were drawn in one session. I took advantage of my husband being away from home for a couple of days to settle down to some serious drawing. The blocks literally appeared overnight. I didn't go to bed and faced the bathroom mirror at 7:00 a.m. the following morning not only with red eyes, but also a very black face. Lead pencil gets everywhere!

Some patterns resemble genuine Pennsylvanian folk art, and some I simply made up as I went along. Once completed, I thought the blocks would translate well into a book and started seeking the fabrics to appropriately depict my own interpretation of the bright colors associated with folk art designs.

A bright and cheerful egg yolk yellow background seemed the perfect setting with small-scale fabrics in primary colors for the appliqué.

The best bit about having one's patterns published is to see others' interpretation of color. I look forward to seeing many tulip quilts and would suggest that a dark background, such as black, dark green, or navy blue, would be an excellent choice and would lead to easier manipulation of the color of the appliqué pieces. Finding the right yellow to appliqué onto a bright yellow background was not easy!

The patterns for the Heart and Tulip blocks in this book will all fit into a 7½"–8" inch block. Most will fit into a 7" block and a few will fit into a 6" block. All will enlarge, some better than others, to fit a 12" block. Each pattern gives alternative suggestions for sizing.

A selection of the 7½" blocks can be used to create a smaller quilt than the one illustrated. A full-size bed quilt could be made repeating only one block. One or two designs might be the ideal solution for the appliquéd blocks in a sampler quilt. The possibilities are endless and suggestions are given for alternative uses of some of the blocks in the pattern section.

Chapter 1
Sewing Techniques

Appliqué

Hand or machine appliqué will work equally well for all the appliqué patterns in this book. The illustrated quilt, FOLK ART AND TULIPS, was made entirely by machine.

The appliqué on the quilt is done by the invisible machine-appliqué technique. Both invisible machine appliqué and hand appliqué require the same methods of preparation for the appliqué pieces. Detailed instructions on how to trim, deal with curves, and make sharp points for hand appliqué can be found in *Masterpiece Appliqué: Little Brown Bird Patterns* by Margaret Docherty and published by the American Quilter's Society.

A rough guide for invisible machine appliqué follows, but novice readers wishing to use this technique should read further. See the Bibliography (page 110).

PHOTO: Margaret Docherty

INVISIBLE MACHINE APPLIQUÉ
Preparing Templates

Cut templates the exact size of the finished motif in freezer paper. Take great care in cutting templates. The finished appliqué will never look good if badly cut or inaccurate templates are used.

NB: Remember, when using freezer paper a reverse image of the motif is produced. Allow for this when preparing templates.

Tip Avoid making a mistake with the templates as follows. Draw the patterns on tracing paper. Write on each pattern, "This side is for marking background fabric. Turn pattern over to draw templates."

Fig. 1. Appliqué pieces with seam allowances turned in, right and wrong sides

Making the Appliqué Pieces

Iron the templates onto the wrong side of the chosen fabric, shiny (sticky) side down. Follow the grain of the fabric whenever possible.

Cut out the appliqué shape in fabric roughly, with a ¼" seam allowance. Trim neatly, leaving a ³⁄₁₆" seam allowance. Clip the curves and sharp angles as needed to prepare the seam allowances for turning in.

A glue stick is the adhesive of choice. Ensure the manufacturer's information states that the glue will wash out with water. Apply glue to the wrong side of the seam allowance. Turn under the seam allowance and adhere to the freezer paper (see figure 1).

Directions for the order of sewing the appliqué pieces are given with each individual pattern.

Using the Sewing Machine

Be kind to your machine. If you treat it well, it will reward you with few problems and good stitches. Keep it clean, oiled, and regularly serviced.

Nine Steps to Remember for Invisible Machine Appliqué

❍ Ensure the machine is well oiled and lint free.

❍ Use a good quality sharp needle. A Micro-tex Sharp size 8/60 needle works well with invisible thread on top and a 60-weight cotton thread in the bobbin. The sharpest possible needle is required for machine appliqué.

❍ Thread the needle with a good quality invisible thread. A fine, supple nylon or polyester is the thread of choice. Use new thread. Old nylon can become stiff and will tangle and break easily.

❍ The thread of choice for the bobbin is a 60-weight cotton or 80-weight machine embroidery thread in a color that matches the background fabric. When overlapping appliqué pieces, change the color of the bobbin thread as necessary to match the underlying appliqué piece.

❍ The tension in the bobbin case may need to be adjusted. It needs to be tighter than the tension for routine sewing. If the stitches from the wrong side of the fabric are showing through to the right side, tighten the bobbin tension.

Tip Buy a spare bobbin case and use it only for machine appliqué. Increase the tension by trial and error. This way you will not upset your sewing machine supplier who dislikes customers fiddling with the bobbin tension.

❍ Use an open-toed embroidery foot. You need to keep your eye on the needle ALL the time. The only way to do this is to have an open space through which to view it.

❍ Use a blind stitch to sew the appliqué in place. Practice the stitch before starting on the appliqué. The stitch length of the blind stitch regulates the distance between the stitches. The stitch width regulates the "bite" taken into the appliqué piece by the invisible thread. To start with, try a stitch width of 1 and a stitch length of .5. With experience, the stitch width can be reduced and the length adjusted as well. Different types of fabric need different widths of stitch. Thicker cottons, especially if patterned, will allow a wider stitch. Judge the width of stitch needed as you proceed.

At the start and finish of stitching, reduce the stitch length to almost zero. This will serve to anchor the thread, which can be cut without tying off.

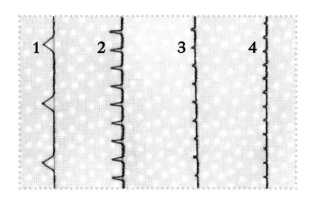

Fig. 2. Blind Stitch.
LINE 1. Regular blind stitch. Stitch length of 2.5, stitch width of 3
LINE 2. Stitch length shortened to .5, regular stitch width of 3
LINE 3. Stitch length of .5, stitch width is shortened to 1
LINE 4. Stitch length of .25, stitch width of 1. This setting is suitable for machine appliqué.

❍ Use the needle-down function all the time if it is available on your machine. The fabric under the presser foot is constantly being repositioned.

❍ Use the knee lift for the presser foot if one is available. It is so much easier to reposition the sewing, done many times in stitching just one small appliqué piece, when both hands are free to manipulate the block.

Tip Keep the stitch length as short as possible, especially on full curves. As for hand appliqué, the closer the stitches are together, the less the likelihood of ugly bulges of fabric along the seam line.

Finishing Off

When all of the appliqué is in place, remove the paper from the back.

Use a pair of appliqué scissors to cut away the background fabric, leaving ¼" seam allowance on the background fabric inside the appliquéd areas. Appliqué scissors have a protective rounded edge on one point that will help to prevent an accidental cut from going through all layers and damaging the appliqué. When stitching one appliqué piece on top of another, before stitching the whole piece to the background fabric, trim the seam allowance inside the smaller appliqué piece and then proceed. Do not remove the papers at this stage. Wait until all the appliqué is stitched to the background fabric (see figure 3).

Once all the background fabric has been cut away, wet the papers thoroughly. Wait a few minutes and the paper will pull away without any resistance. If resistance is felt, add a little more water and try again. A pair of fine-pointed forceps helps remove the papers without distorting the appliqué. Allow the appliqué to dry a little and press while it is still damp.

Raw-edge appliqué without a turned edge can be accomplished with a satin stitch or blanket stitch and a fabric stabilizer (see the Bibliography, page 110).

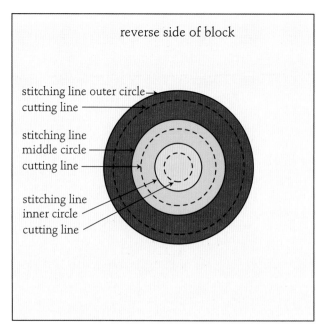

reverse side of block

stitching line outer circle
cutting line

stitching line
middle circle
cutting line

stitching line
inner circle
cutting line

Fig. 3. Cutting away the background fabric

Hearts & Tulips ⁂ Margaret Docherty

Quilting

The illustrated quilt, FOLK ART AND TULIPS, was machine quilted.

Patterns are given in the pattern section for the quilting motifs used in the blocks and the feathers used in the border.

The background was fine-stipple quilted using a 60-weight cotton thread on the top and in the bobbin. This would not be recommended for hand quilting. A cross-hatch quilting pattern would be more appropriate.

The motifs and feathers were stitched with a heavier weight machine embroidery thread on top and a matching color of polyester bobbin thread in the bobbin. The feathers and motifs can equally well be hand quilted.

Stuffing the Quilting Motifs

The feathers and motifs were padded with five layers of batting.

Padded Machine Quilting

The padding is put in place after marking the quilting pattern on the quilt top but before the batting and lining are in place.

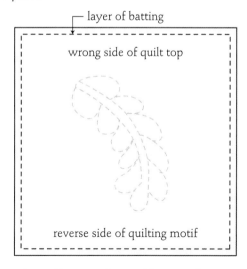

Fig. 4. Putting the padding in place

Add as many layers of batting as you wish, cut to size, and place behind each motif on the quilt top.

Hold in place with basting glue or basting stitches.

Machine stitch the batting in place along the marked quilting lines. Use a water-soluble thread in the top and an ordinary bobbin thread in the bobbin.

Carefully trim the batting away from the edges of the temporary stitching.

Tip Be very careful not to get any water on the quilt or the stitches holding the stuffing in place will disappear.

Make a quilt sandwich by adding the batting and quilt backing. Baste the three layers together with basting pins, spray basting adhesive, or basting stitches.

Stitch over the quilting lines of the feathers and motifs again, this time with a permanent thread on the top of the machine, stitching through all three layers of the quilt.

After adding a binding to your finished quilt, wash the quilt and the first line of stitching on the feathers and motifs will disappear. The bobbin thread will not come through to the right side of the fabric.

Hand quilting can be stuffed with trapunto wool after the quilting is complete.

— layer of batting

wrong side of quilt top

stitching line

cutting line —
as close to stitching
as possible

Fig. 5. Cutting away the surplus batting from wrong side of quilt top

Close-up of stuffed quilting motif

Close-up of appliqué, 4 blocks together

FOLK ART AND TULIPS, 68" x 68", made by the author

Chapter 2
Size, Materials, Cutting, and Quilt Construction

BLOCK SIZES 7½" AND 9¾"
QUILT SIZE 68" X 68"

Main Fabrics

Materials, based on 42" wide fabric

Extra length is allowed on borders and blocks where appliqué may distort the fabric.

5¾ yards of egg-yolk yellow background (see cutting instructions)
1 yard dark red small-scale print
1 yard medium red small-scale print
2 yards medium blue small-scale print (includes binding)
½ yard medium green small-scale print
76" x 76" of batting
4¼ yards of lining (quilt backing)

The dark red fabric was used for the half-circle border edgings as well as in the appliquéd blocks. The medium red was used for all the appliqué in the borders as well as in the blocks. The blue fabric was used in the appliqué and for the binding. *These fabrics will be referred to in the pattern section as main dark red, main medium red, and main blue fabrics.*

The green fabric was used for all the stems and leaves of the border appliqué. The half yard is sufficient for it to be used in several of the block patterns as well.

Cutting diagram

Scraps of Fabrics

The original quilt used 94 different fabrics. Aim to have a fat quarter or fat eighth of the following fabrics. Unless stated otherwise, select a small-scale print. Suggestions for the color of additional smaller pieces of fabric used for the appliqué are found alongside the appliqué patterns in Chapter 3.

Blue: 1 light, 2 medium, 1 dark, 1 light check or stripe, 1 large-scale print (for vases)

Red: 1 light (red & white print), 2 medium, 1 dark, 1 stripe, 1 check (red & white)

Pink red: 1 dark, 1 medium.

Orange red: 1 dark, 1 medium

Pink: 1 medium.

Yellow: 1 stripe, 1 multi-dot, 3 dark (Use one exclusively for the tulips on the borders and in Blocks 11 and 20.)

Green: 1 light, 2 medium, 1 dark, 1 check

½ yard red rickrack

Solids: green, medium blue, medium dark blue, bright yellow

Cutting

From 3¼ yards of the background fabric, cut the borders and corner blocks as shown in the cutting diagram:

4 strips 11" x 47", cut lengthwise
4 strips 2½" x 69", cut lengthwise
4 blocks 11" x 11"

From the remaining background yardage, cut 36 blocks 9" x 9".

You'll need 282" of bias binding. Cut 2½" strips from ¾ yard of the main blue fabric.

Quilt Dimensions

36 BLOCKS

cut 9" x 9"

trim to 8" x 8" when appliqué completed

finished size = 7½" x 7½"

4 CORNER BLOCKS

cut 11" x 11"

trim to 10¼" x 10¼" when appliqué completed

finished size = 9¾" x 9¾"

INNER BORDER

cut 11" x 47"

trim to 10¼" x 45½"

finished size = 9¾" x 45"

OUTER BORDER

cut 2½" x 69"

trim to 2" wide

finished width = 1½"

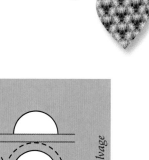

○ Draw 146 circles of 1½" diameter on freezer paper. Cut out the circles and cut across the middle of each to give 2 half circles.

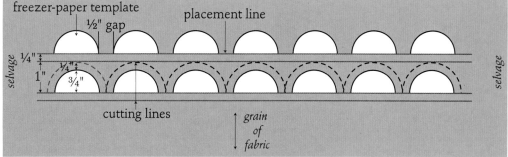

Fig. 6. Cutting the dark red half circles

○ Draw lines on the wrong side of the main red fabric as shown (see figure 6). Use these lines as placement lines for the freezer-paper half circles. Place the straight edges of the semicircles on these lines. Draw another line ¼" below the placement line. This is the cutting line. To allow for the seam allowance on the curved area, leave ½" between the semicircles. From the main dark red fabric cut 292 half circles. Prepare the fabric half circles for appliqué, leaving the straight edge unturned (see figure 7).

Fig. 7. Detail of prepared half circles

Quilt Construction

See figure 8.

❍ Appliqué 36 blocks. The 36 blocks used in the quilt plus two bonus blocks are given in Chapter 3. General instructions for appliqué are in Chapter 1 and specific instructions for each block are with the patterns in Chapter 3.

❍ As each block is completed, rinse out any markings and press. Trim the block to 8" x 8" (finished size = 7½" x 7½").

❍ Join the blocks in 6 rows of 6 with ¼" seams. Use your method of choice to press the seam allowances. In FOLK ART AND TULIPS, the seams were pressed open, with the first and last ¼" of each seam allowance left unstitched. This gives a flatter finish and less obvious seam lines on the right side of the quilt. Alternatively, press the seam allowance to one side.

❍ Appliqué 4 wide border strips and stitch the half circle trim to the inner edge of each wide border, aligning the raw edges (refer to the photograph of the quilt).

❍ The finished length of the border is 45". Thirty half circles are used along each edge. The finished fabric half circles measure slightly more than 1½" and some adjustment is needed to fit them onto the seam line. Lay the border out on a flat surface. Mark the center and the end points, each being 22½" from the center. Starting at the center, position 15 half circles on each side. Overlap as necessary and glue-baste in place before stitching.

❍ Rinse out any markings. Press the finished border and trim to 10¼" x 45½" (finished size = 9¾" x 45").

❍ Appliqué the 4 corner blocks.

❍ Rinse out any markings. Press the finished blocks and trim to 10¼" x 10¼" (finished size = 9¾" x 9¾").

❍ Join the corner blocks to either end of the top and bottom border strips. Press the seam allowances, either open or to one side.

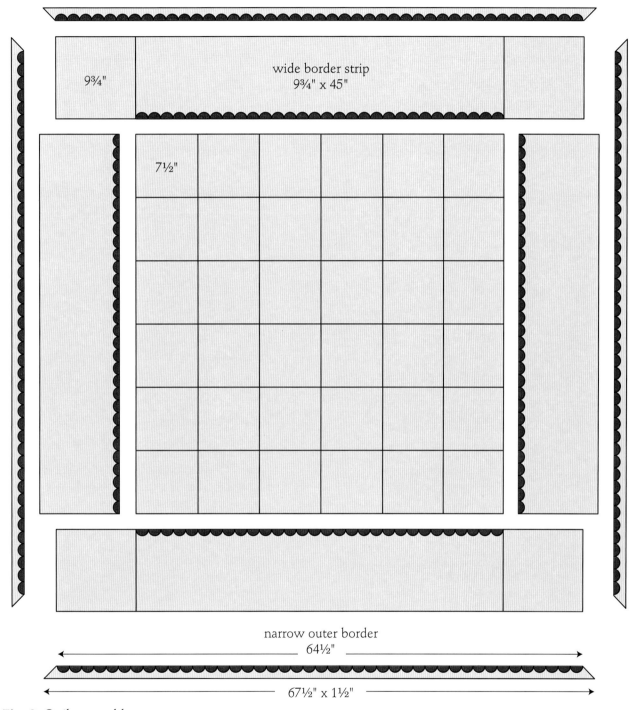

Fig. 8. Quilt assembly

○ Stitch the side borders to the sides of the body of the quilt.

○ Stitch the top and bottom border units, with the corner units attached, to the side borders and the body of the quilt (refer to the quilt assembly on page 23). Press the seam allowances.

○ Stitch the half circle trim to the inner edge of each narrow outer border, matching the seam lines. The inner edge of this border measures 64½". Position 43 half circles along the seam line, with the center of one half circle matching the center of the border. Overlap as necessary to fit.

NB: The outer border of the illustrated quilt used one less half circle on each side—42 instead of 43 half circles—which eliminated overlapping of half circles.

○ Rinse out the marking pen if necessary. Press the finished borders and trim to a width of 2" (finished width = 1½").

○ The end seams are mitered (see page 25). The finished inner edge of the outer border is 64½" long and the finished outer edge of the outer border is 67½" long.

○ Join each border to the quilt top and finally stitch the corner diagonal seam allowances together.

○ Follow instructions in Chapter 1 for stuffed machine quilting (pages 15–16).

○ Make the quilt lining (backing). Ensure the background fabric has no folds or wrinkles in it before cutting. Press if necessary. Cut 2 panels of background fabric, each 74" long. Cut one panel in half, longitudinally (lengthwise). Join the 3 panels as shown in figure 9. Press seam allowances to one side.

○ Use a quilt batting at least the size of the quilt backing. Leave the batting opened and unfolded for a day or so before it is needed to remove creases.

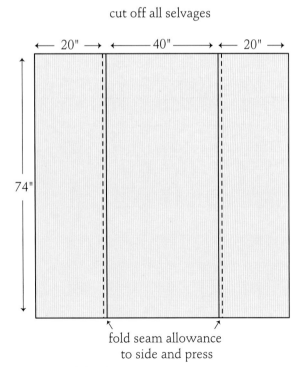

cut off all selvages

← 20" → ← 40" → ← 20" →

74"

fold seam allowance
to side and press

Fig. 9. Quilt backing

Mitering Borders

The inner edge of a border will have a finished length the same as that of the quilt body to which it is attached. The outer finished length will extend beyond this length by the width of the border at each end. Example: For a 70" wide quilt with an 8" border, the finished outer edge will be 86".

Mark the corner seams on each border as follows:

○ On the wrong side of the borders, measure in ¼" from the edges to mark the seam lines at both ends, as shown below. Mark off a square at each end. The square is equal to the width of the border, 8".

○ Check the distance between A–A and B–B on each border strip. A–A should be 70", and B–B should be 86".

○ Mark diagonal A–B lines as shown. These are the stitching lines.

○ Join all four borders to the quilt between points A–A.

○ To complete the border, join seams A–B to A–B on adjacent borders.

○ Trim away excess fabric and press seam allowance to one side.

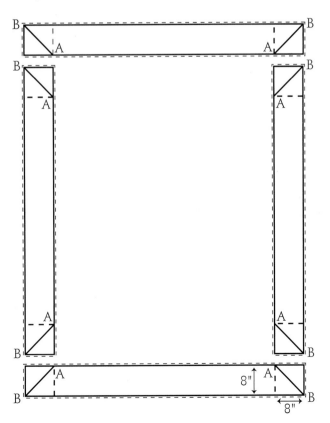

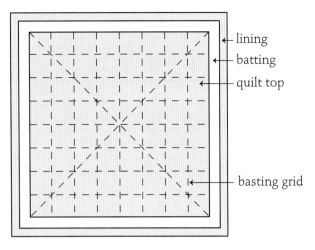

Fig. 10. Quilt basting

○ Make a quilt sandwich starting with the lining fabric placed the wrong side up. Smooth it out and place the batting on top. Next place the quilt top, right side up, on top of the batting. Baste and trim the spare edges of batting and quilt backing (figure 10).

○ Quilt the completed quilt top. Suggested quilting patterns are given alongside the appliqué patterns in Chapter 3.

○ When the quilting is in place, add the blue binding. The given width allows for a double-fold binding of finished width ½".

○ Add a quilt label to the reverse side of your quilt (see figure 11).

Fig. 11. Quilt label

Chapter 3
The Patterns

Introduction

❍ The patterns are identified with a number and a name.

❍ The appliqué pieces are shown in solid lines.

❍ The suggested quilting motifs for each block are shown in broken lines.

❍ Each pattern is marked with letters and numbers.

❍ The *numbers* indicate the order of appliqué.

❍ The *letters* indicate pieces of appliqué that are stitched to another piece of appliqué before attaching the completed piece to the background fabric.

❍ Full instructions for using the numbers and letters are given in the first three blocks. Block 32, The Love Birds, and block 34, Tulip Bells, have a more complex order of appliqué and full instructions are given alongside those patterns as well.

❍ Fabric yardage is given in Chapter 2 (page 19).

❍ Suggested fabric selection is given alongside each pattern.

❍ Alternate suggestions for use of the blocks and for resizing them are also given with each pattern. Also consider a two-block quilt that has appliqué blocks alternating with pieced blocks (see the Bibliography, page 110).

❍ In all patterns, x marks the center of the pattern, to be aligned with the center of the background fabric square.

❍ See Chapter 1 for instructions on how to prepare appliqué pieces and sewing suggestions.

PART 1: *Single Blooms*

This comprises six patterns with only one tulip in the design.

These are the simplest of the appliqué blocks.

One or two could be used in a sampler quilt with 6" blocks.

Where appropriate, instructions for reduction and enlargement of the blocks are given.

Block 1 *Simple Tulip*

This is the simplest of all the designs.

Fabric Requirements

Background fabric

Small scraps of quilting weight cotton fabrics

    1 red

    1 yellow stripe

    1 blue

    1 dark green

ORDER OF APPLIQUÉ

○ First stitch the small heart A to the striped yellow petal B. Cut away the background fabric behind the heart leaving ¼" seam allowance. Do not remove the freezer paper at this stage. Wait until all the appliqué is in place.

○ Stitch the appliqué pieces in the order given on the pattern, numbers 1–4.

○ Stitch the stem, leaves, blue circles, and blue petals to background fabric.

○ Stitch the striped yellow petal, with red heart already attached, to the blue petals. If using the invisible machine-appliqué technique, consider using a blue thread in the bobbin.

○ Stitch the final piece, the red outer petal.

○ Remove papers and press as described in Chapter 1 (page 14).

EMBROIDERY

Hand embroider stems between the blue circles and the top of the tulip in stem stitch.

ALTERNATIVE USES FOR BLOCK

Ideal in a 7½" to 8" block.

Fits comfortably in a 6" block.

Not recommended for enlargement.

Block 1 *Simple Tulip*

Block 2 *Chunky Tulip*

Hint: The leaves can be cut as one unit, which will eliminate the possibility of raw edges at the end of the leaves protruding beyond the stem.

Fabric Requirements

Background fabric

Main blue fabric

Small scraps of quilting weight cotton fabrics

    1 solid red

    1 red & white

    1 yellow

    1 medium pink

    1 green

ORDER OF APPLIQUÉ

○ First stitch the pink sepal A to the larger solid red sepal B. Cut away the background fabric behind the pink sepal leaving a scant ¼" seam allowance. Do not remove the freezer paper at this stage. Wait until all the appliqué is in place.

○ Stitch the appliqué pieces in the order given on the pattern, numbers 1–6

○ Stitch the leaves and the blue petals to the background fabric.

○ Stitch the stem to the background fabric. Stitch the patterned red petals to the blue petals. If using the invisible machine-appliqué technique, consider using a blue thread in the bobbin.

○ Stitch the solid red sepal, with the pink sepal attached. If using the invisible machine-appliqué technique, consider changing the color of the bobbin thread when stitching over the petals. Stitch the red patterned frilled edge at the base of the stem to the background fabric.

○ Stitch the blue pieces at the base of the stem to the patterned red frills.

○ Stitch the yellow center to the petals.

○ Add the last appliqué piece, the solid red base of the flower holder.

EMBROIDERY

Hand embroider stamens with stem stitch and French knots.

ALTERNATIVE USES FOR BLOCK

Ideal in a 7½" to 8" block.

Minimum block size is 7".

Photocopy at 85% for a 6" block.

Photocopy at 170% for a 12" block.

Block 2 *Chunky Tulip*

Block 3 *Stenciled Tulip*

ORDER OF APPLIQUÉ

○ First stitch the light green leaf pieces A to the larger darker leaf pieces B. Stitch the patterned blue heart A to the larger solid blue heart B. Cut away the background fabric leaving a scant ¼" seam allowance. Do not remove the freezer paper at this stage. Wait until all the appliqué is in place.

○ Stitch the appliqué pieces in the order given on the pattern, numbers 1–3.

○ Stitch all petal pieces marked 2, the stem, and the leaves to the background fabric.

○ Stitch the center of the flower and the large heart in place. Add the blue ovals around the heart.

Fabric Requirements

Background fabric

Small scraps of quilting weight cotton fabrics

    1 dark orange-red

    1 medium orange-red

    1 dark or medium green

    1 light green

    1 solid blue

    1 patterned blue

ALTERNATIVE USES FOR BLOCK

Ideal in a 7½" to 8" block.

Minimum block size is 7½".

Photocopy at 80% for a 6" block.

Photocopy at 160% for a 12" block.

The heart motif without the flower can be used in a variety of appliqué projects.

Block 3: *Stenciled Tulip*

Block 4 *Egghead Tulip*

Fabric Requirements

Background fabric

Small scraps of quilting weight cotton fabrics

    1 dark red

    1 medium red

    1 light red (red & white patterned)

    1 patterned yellow

    1 blue

    1 medium or dark green

    1 light green

ORDER OF APPLIQUÉ

◯ Stitch pieces marked A to pieces marked B as described in blocks 1–3.

◯ Stitch the appliqué pieces in the order given on the pattern, numbers 1–9.

EMBROIDERY

Hand embroider stems between the blue circles and the top of the tulip in stem stitch.

ALTERNATIVE USES FOR BLOCK

Ideal in a 7½" to 8" block.

Photocopy at 90% for a 6" block.

Photocopy at 180% for a 12" block.

Block 4: *Egghead Tulip*

Block 5 *Frilly Tulip*

Fabric Requirements

Background fabric

Small scraps of quilting weight cotton fabrics

    1 dark red

    1 dark pink

    1 medium pink

    1 medium-dark blue

    1 light blue

    1 green

ORDER OF APPLIQUÉ

○ Stitch the heart marked A to the heart marked B as described in blocks 1–3.

○ Stitch the appliqué pieces in the order given on the pattern, numbers 1–8.

ALTERNATIVE USES FOR BLOCK

Ideal in a 7½" to 8" block.

Photocopy at 90% for a 6" block. If the bottom leaves are trimmed back a little, the pattern will fit into a 6" block without resizing.

Photocopy at 180% for a 12" block.

Block 5: *Frilly Tulip*

Block 6 *Lyre Tulip*

Fabric Requirements

Background fabric

Main medium red fabric

Small scraps of quilting weight cotton fabrics

    1 dark red

    1 pink

    1 medium-dark blue solid

    1 patterned blue

    1 green solid

    1 green check

    1 bright yellow

ORDER OF APPLIQUÉ

◯ Stitch pieces marked A to pieces marked B as described in blocks 1–3.

◯ Stitch the appliqué pieces in the order given on the pattern, numbers 1–5.

EMBROIDERY

Hand embroider stamens with stem stitch and French knots.

ALTERNATIVE USES FOR BLOCK

Minimum block size is 7½".

Photocopy at 80% for 6" block.

Photocopy at 160% for a 12" block.

Block 6: *Lyre Tulip*

PART 2: *A Bakers Dozen: Thirteen Bunches of Tulips*

These thirteen blocks have more detail than the previous six. Buds and small tulips are added to the main large tulip.

These blocks will enlarge well to fit a 12" block. Technically, they will be more challenging to sew if reduced to fit into a 6" block.

Block 7 *Cute Tulip*

Fabric Requirements

Background fabric

Main dark red fabric

Main medium red fabric

Small scraps of quilting weight cotton fabrics

    1 red & white check

    1 medium-dark blue solid

    1 light-blue check or stripe

    1 green

    1 bright yellow

ORDER OF APPLIQUÉ

○ Stitch pieces marked A to pieces marked B as described in blocks 1–3. Stitch the heart B to the heart C.

○ Stitch the appliqué pieces in the order given on the pattern, numbers 1 5.

EMBROIDERY

Hand embroider stamens with stem stitch and French knots.

ALTERNATIVE USES FOR BLOCK

Minimum block size is 7".

Photocopy at 80% for 6" block.

Photocopy at 170% for a 12" block.

This block that will successfully set diagonally.

Block 7: *Cute Tulip*

Block 8 *Versatile Tulip*

Fabric Requirements

Background fabric

Main dark red fabric

Small scraps of quilting weight cotton fabrics

    1 medium red

    1 medium-dark blue solid

    1 patterned blue

    1 green

    1 dark yellow

Order of Appliqué

○ Stitch the heart A to the heart B as described in blocks 1–3.

○ Stitch the appliqué pieces in the order given on the pattern, numbers 1–5.

Alternative Uses for Block

Minimum block size is 7".

Photocopy at 80% for 6" block.

Photocopy at 170% for a 12" block.

This pattern lends itself to a diagonal setting with 4 blocks grouped together (see figure below).

A suggested alternative use for Block 8, The Versatile Tulip

Block 8: *Versatile Tulip*

Block 9 *Long Tall Sally Tulip*

Fabric Requirements

Background fabric

Main medium red fabric (outer heart)

Small scraps of quilting weight cotton fabrics

1 red with yellow dot

1 dark blue

1 medium blue solid

1 green

1 yellow multi–dot

Order of Appliqué

○ Stitch pieces marked A to pieces marked B as described in blocks 1–3.

○ Stitch the heart B to the heart C.

○ Stitch the appliqué pieces in the order given on the pattern, numbers 1–4.

Embroidery

Hand embroider stems in stem stitch between the blue circles and the blue hearts and between the red circles and the small red tulips. Optionally, join the small blue hearts to the main stem with stem stitch.

Alternative Uses for Block

Minimum block size is 7½".

Photocopy at 80% for 6" block.

Photocopy at 160% for a 12" block.

This block is taller than it is wide. If enlarged, it will look better in a rectangular block than a square one.

Block 9: *Long Tall Sally Tulip*

Block 10 *Wilting Stem Tulip*

Fabric Requirements

Background fabric

Main medium red fabric

Small scraps of quilting weight cotton fabrics

    1 dark red

    1 red with yellow dot

    1 red & white stripe

    1 medium blue

    1 dark green

    1 light green

ORDER OF APPLIQUÉ

❍ Stitch pieces marked A to pieces marked B as described in blocks 1–3.

❍ Stitch the appliqué pieces in the order given on the pattern, numbers 1–5.

EMBROIDERY

Hand embroider stamens with stem stitch and French knots.

ALTERNATIVE USES FOR BLOCK

Minimum block size is 7".

Photocopy at 85% for 6" block.

Photocopy at 170% for a 12" block.

Block 10: *Wilting Stem Tulip*

Block 11 *Handsome Tulip*

ORDER OF APPLIQUÉ

○ Stitch pieces marked A to pieces marked B as described in blocks 1–3.

○ Stitch the heart B to the heart C.

○ Stitch the appliqué pieces in the order given on the pattern, numbers 1–4.

ALTERNATIVE USES FOR BLOCK

Minimum block size is 7½".

Photocopy at 80% for 6" block.

Photocopy at 160% for a 12" block. This is another block that would look well set diagonally in a group of 4.

Fabric Requirements

Background fabric

Main medium red fabric

Main blue fabric

Small scraps of quilting weight cotton fabrics

    1 medium red (middle heart)

    1 red & white check

    1 medium-dark blue stripe

    1 dark green

    1 light green

    1 bright yellow. This yellow is used again in the border tulips. Ensure you have sufficient yardage.

Block 11: *Handsome Tulip*

Block 12 *Dainty Tulip*

Fabric Requirements

Background fabric

Small scraps of quilting weight cotton fabrics

    1 medium red solid

    1 white & red

    1 medium blue

    1 dark blue

    1 green

    1 bright yellow

Order of Appliqué

◯ Stitch pieces marked A to pieces marked B as described in blocks 1–3.

◯ Stitch the appliqué pieces in the order given on the pattern, numbers 1–4.

Embroidery

Join the green circles to the dark blue hearts with hand embroidered stem stitch. Use stem stitch and French knots for the stamens.

Alternative Uses for Block

Minimum block size is 7".

Photocopy at 85% for 6" block.

Photocopy at 170% for a 12" block.

Block 12: *Dainty Tulip*

Block 13 *Medusa Tulip*

Fabric Requirements

Background fabric

Small scraps of quilting weight cotton fabrics

    1 orange-red

    1 red & white check

    1 medium-dark blue

    1 blue stripe (flower pot)

    1 very dark green

    1 medium green

    1 bright yellow

ORDER OF APPLIQUÉ

○ Stitch pieces marked A to pieces marked B as described in blocks 1–3.

○ Stitch the appliqué pieces in the order given on the pattern, numbers 1–6.

○ The stripe across the flower pot on the pattern is optional.

EMBROIDERY

Hand embroider stamens with stem stitch and French knots.

ALTERNATIVE USES FOR BLOCK

Minimum block size is 7½".

Photocopy at 80% for 6" block.

Photocopy at 160% for a 12" block. This block will enlarge well.

Block 13: *Medusa Tulip*

Block 14 *Architectural Tulip*

Fabric Requirements

Background fabric

Main medium red fabric

Small scraps of quilting weight cotton fabrics

    1 red with yellow dot

    1 medium blue

    1 light blue

    1 medium-dark green

    1 yellow stripe

ORDER OF APPLIQUÉ

○ Stitch the heart A to the heart B as described in blocks 1–3.

○ Stitch the appliqué pieces in the order given on the pattern, numbers 1–5.

EMBROIDERY

Hand embroider stamens with stem stitch and French knots. Join the blue circles to the top of the tulip with stem stitch.

ALTERNATIVE USES FOR BLOCK

Minimum block size is 7½".

Photocopy at 80% for 6" block.

Photocopy at 160% for a 12" block.

Block 14: *Architectural Tulip*

Block 15 *Tulips and Bulb*

Fabric Requirements

Background fabric

Main medium red fabric

Small scraps of quilting weight cotton fabrics

    1 white & red

    1 medium blue

    1 light green

    1 dark green

    1 bright yellow

ORDER OF APPLIQUÉ

○ Stitch pieces marked A to pieces marked B as described in blocks 1–3.

○ Stitch the appliqué pieces in the order given on the pattern, numbers 1–7.

ALTERNATIVE USES FOR BLOCK

Minimum block size is 7".

Photocopy at 85% for 6" block.

Photocopy at 170% for a 12" block.

Block 15: *Tulips and Bulb*

Block 16 *Blue-Eyed Tulip*

Fabric Requirements

Background fabric

Small scraps of quilting weight cotton fabrics

    1 red & dark pink

    1 red narrow stripe

    1 medium blue

    1 blue stripe

    1 dark green

ORDER OF APPLIQUÉ

○ Stitch pieces marked A to pieces marked B as described in blocks 1–3.

○ Stitch the appliqué pieces in the order given on the pattern, numbers 1–5.

EMBROIDERY

Hand embroider stamens with stem stitch and French knots.

ALTERNATIVE USES FOR BLOCK

Minimum block size is 7½".

Photocopy at 80% for 6" block.

Photocopy at 160% for a 12" block.

Recommended for 12" block.

Block 16: *Blue-Eyed Tulip*

Block 17 *Double Tulip*

Fabric Requirements

Background fabric

Main blue (heart)

Small scraps of quilting weight cotton fabrics

    1 red & dark pink

    1 dark pink (heart)

    1 white & red

    1 medium blue

    1 light green

    1 dark green

    1 mustard yellow

ORDER OF APPLIQUÉ

◯ Stitch pieces marked A to pieces marked B as described in blocks 1–3.

◯ Stitch the appliqué pieces in the order given on the pattern, numbers 1–5.

ALTERNATIVE USES FOR BLOCK

Minimum block size is 7½".

Photocopy at 80% for 6" block.

Photocopy at 160% for a 12" block. Recommended for 12" block.

Block 17: *Double Tulip*

Block 18 *Dutch Clogs Tulip*

Fabric Requirements

Background fabric

Small scraps of quilting weight cotton fabrics

1 medium red

1 white & red

1 medium blue

1 medium green

1 dark green with red spot

1 yellow stripe

1 black & red check

1 black & white check

ORDER OF APPLIQUÉ

○ Stitch pieces marked A to pieces marked B as described in blocks 1–3.

○ Stitch the appliqué pieces in the order given on the pattern, numbers 1–7. The frilled trim on top of bowl is optional.

EMBROIDERY

Hand embroider stamens with stem stitch and French knots.

ALTERNATIVE USES FOR BLOCK

Minimum block size is 7½".

Photocopy at 80% for 6" block.

Photocopy at 160% for a 12" block. Recommended for 12" block.

Block 18: *Dutch Clogs Tulip*

Block 19 *Heart's Tongue Tulip*

Fabric Requirements

Background fabric

Small scraps of quilting weight cotton fabrics

 1 dark red

 1 dark pink

 1 medium pink

 1 medium blue

 1 blue with large-scale pattern

  (flower pot)

 1 dark green

 1 light green

 1 bright yellow

ORDER OF APPLIQUÉ

○ Stitch pieces marked A to pieces marked B as described in blocks 1–3.

○ Stitch the appliqué pieces in the order given on the pattern, numbers 1–7. The striped trim on the bowl is optional.

EMBROIDERY

Hand embroider stems between the blue circles and the top of the tulip in stem stitch.

ALTERNATIVE USES FOR BLOCK

Minimum block size is 7".

Photocopy at 85% for 6" block.

Photocopy at 170% for a 12" block. Recommended for 12" block.

Block 19: *Heart's Tongue Tulip*

PART 3: *The Tulip Vases*

There are three vases of tulips in the quilt. There is another pattern for a vase of tulips in the last pattern section, the bonus blocks—two extra blocks that are not in the quilt.

Block 20 *Bud Vase of Tulips*

ORDER OF APPLIQUÉ

○ Stitch pieces marked A to pieces marked B as described in blocks 1–3.

○ Stitch the appliqué pieces in the order given on the pattern, numbers 1–7.

EMBROIDERY

Hand embroider stamens with stem stitch and French knots.

ALTERNATIVE USES FOR BLOCK

Minimum block size is 7½".

Photocopy at 80% for 6" block.

Photocopy at 160% for a 12" block. Recommended for 12" block.

Fabric Requirements

Background fabric

Main medium red fabric

Small scraps of quilting weight cotton fabrics

    1 medium blue

    1 blue with large-scale pattern
       (for vase)

    1 medium green

    1 bright yellow. This yellow is used again in the border tulips. Ensure you have sufficient yardage to continue. A fat quarter will suffice.

Block 20: *Bud Vase of Tulips*

Block 21 *Tulip Tree*

Fabric Requirements

Background fabric

Main blue fabric

Small scraps of quilting weight cotton fabrics

1 orange red

1 medium green

1 red & black large-scale print

ORDER OF APPLIQUÉ

○ Stitch the appliqué pieces in the order given on the pattern, numbers 1–3.

EMBROIDERY

Hand embroider stamens with stem stitch and French knots.

ALTERNATIVE USES FOR BLOCK

This pattern will fit very snugly into a 6" block. It will enlarge equally well to fit a 12" block.

Photocopy at 185% for a 12" block.

Block 21: *Tulip Tree*

Block 22 *Black Tulips*

Fabric Requirements

Background fabric

Small scraps of quilting weight cotton fabrics

- 1 dark red
- 1 dark pink
- 1 light green
- 1 medium blue
- 1 medium blue large-scale print
- 1 striped yellow print

ORDER OF APPLIQUÉ

◯ Stitch pieces marked A to pieces marked B as described in blocks 1–3.

◯ Stitch the appliqué pieces in the order given on the pattern, numbers 1–4.

EMBROIDERY

Hand embroider stamens with stem stitch and French knots.

ALTERNATIVE USES FOR BLOCK

Minimum block size is 7½". Reducing block size is not recommended.

Photocopy at 160% for a 12" block. This block will enlarge very well.

Block 22: *Black Tulips*

PART 4: *Five of the Best*

The following five blocks are the most versatile in the book. They are symmetrical in shape and reach to the corners of the block. They are ideal for enlarging, they will sit diagonally in a block, and each could be used for a one-block quilt. A similar block (Block 37) can be found in the bonus blocks section.

Block 23 *Gingham and Rose Tulip*

ORDER OF APPLIQUÉ

◯ Stitch pieces marked A to pieces marked B as described in blocks 1–3.

◯ Stitch the middle rose section B to the outer rose section C.

◯ Stitch the appliqué pieces in the order given on the pattern, numbers 1–5.

Fabric Requirements

Background fabric
Small scraps of quilting weight cotton fabrics
   1 dark pink
   1 dark pink check
   1 medium green
   1 medium blue
   1 bright yellow

EMBROIDERY

Hand embroider stamens with stem stitch and French knots.

ALTERNATIVE USES FOR BLOCK

Minimum block size is 7½".

Photocopy at 160% for a 12" block. Enlargement is recommended.

Pattern can also be set diagonally in a block.

Block 23: *Gingham and Rose Tulip*

Block 24 *Old-Fashioned Tulip*

Fabric Requirements

Background fabric

Small scraps of quilting weight cotton fabrics

    1 dark pink

    1 red & white stripe

    1 light green

    1 medium blue

    1 orange yellow

ORDER OF APPLIQUÉ

○ Stitch the appliqué pieces in the order given on the pattern, numbers 1–3.

ALTERNATIVE USES FOR BLOCK

Minimum block size is 6½".

Photocopy at 90% for a 6" block.

Photocopy at 180% for a 12" block. Enlargement is recommended.

Pattern can also be set diagonally in a block.

Block 24: *Old-Fashioned Tulip*

Block 25 *Czech Me Out Tulip*

Fabric Requirements

Background fabric

Small scraps of quilting weight cotton fabrics

    1 dark orange-red

    1 red & white check

    1 orange-yellow patterned

    1 medium green

    1 medium blue

    1 blue check

    1 bright yellow

ORDER OF APPLIQUÉ

○ Stitch pieces marked A to pieces marked B as described in blocks 1–3.

○ Stitch the appliqué pieces in the order given on the pattern, numbers 1–5.

EMBROIDERY

Hand embroider stamens with stem stitch and French knots.

ALTERNATIVE USES FOR BLOCK

Minimum block size is 7½".

Photocopy at 160% for a 12" block. Enlargement is recommended.

Pattern can also be set diagonally in a block.

Block 25: *Czech Me Out Tulip*

Block 26 *Dotty Tulip*

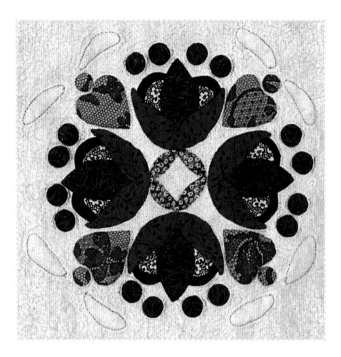

Fabric Requirements

Background fabric

Main blue fabric

Main dark red fabric

Small scraps of quilting weight cotton fabrics

1 very dark red

1 dark pink

1 medium green

1 dark yellow

ORDER OF APPLIQUÉ

○ Stitch the appliqué pieces in the order given on the pattern, numbers 1–6.

ALTERNATIVE USES FOR BLOCK

Minimum block size is 7".

Photocopy at 85% for 6" block.

Photocopy at 170% for a 12" block. Enlargement is recommended.

Pattern can also be set diagonally in a block.

Block 26: *Dotty Tulip*

Block 27 *Exotic Tulip*

Fabric Requirements

Background fabric

Main blue fabric

Small scraps of quilting weight cotton fabrics

    1 dark red

    1 dark pink

    1 medium green

    1 yellow stripe

ORDER OF APPLIQUÉ

   ○ Stitch pieces marked A to pieces marked B as described in blocks 1–3.

   ○ Stitch the appliqué pieces in the order given on the pattern, numbers 1–8.

EMBROIDERY

Hand embroider stamens with stem stitch and French knots.

ALTERNATIVE USES FOR BLOCK

This design will just squeeze into a 6" block. A better effect would be to reduce the pattern, photocopying at 90–95%.

Photocopy at 185% for a 12" block. Enlargement is recommended.

Pattern can also be set diagonally in a block.

6 C

7 B

1 A

5

3

2

8

4

2

Block 27: *Exotic Tulip*

PART 5: *The Distelfink Blocks or Good Luck and Happiness for All*

These eight blocks all have good luck birds. Traditionally the distelfink, or goldfinch, was thought to act as a magical talisman, bringing good luck. Hearts and tulips regularly appeared with the distelfink in Pennsylvania Dutch folk art, symbolizing love, faith, and birth.

Block 28 *The Dove*

Fabric Requirements

Background fabric

Main medium red fabric

    (center of bird's wing)

Small scraps of quilting weight cotton fabrics

    1 dark blue

    1 medium blue

    1 light blue

    1 medium green

    1 bright yellow

    1 orange print

    1 deep orange-red

    1 light brown (beak)

ORDER OF APPLIQUÉ

○ Stitch pieces marked A to pieces marked B as described in blocks 1–3. Stitch wing part B to wing part C.

○ Stitch the appliqué pieces in the order given on the pattern, numbers 1–10.

EMBROIDERY

Hand embroider stamens with stem stitch and French knots. Work the stems and bird's feet in stem stitch. Work the bird's eye in black satin stitch. Use stem stitch to divide the beak.

ALTERNATIVE USES FOR BLOCK

Minimum block size is 7".

Photocopy at 85% for 6" block.

Photocopy at 170% for a 12" block.

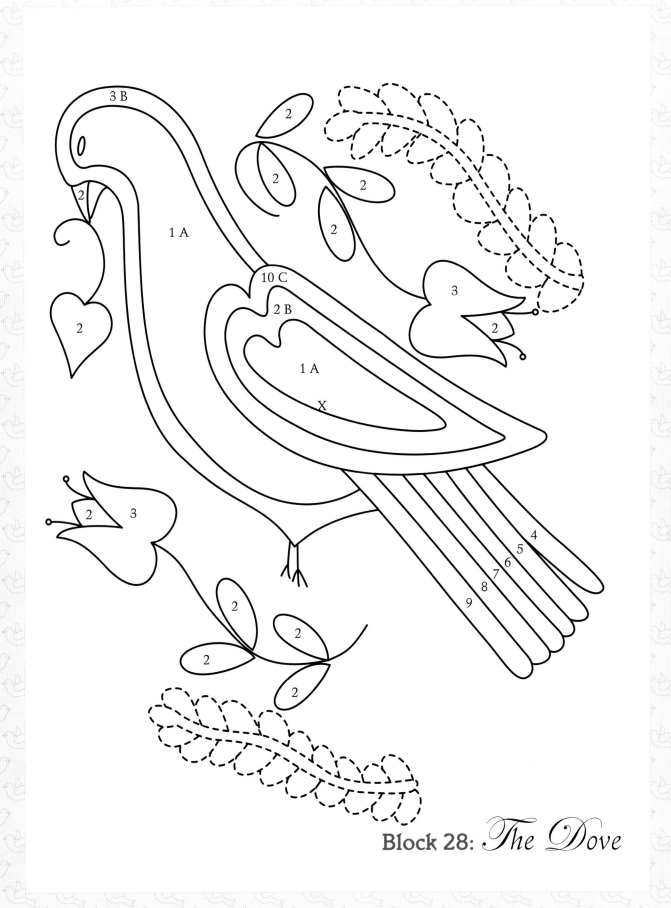

Block 28: *The Dove*

Block 29 *In the Shade*

Fabric Requirements

Background fabric

Small scraps of quilting weight cotton fabrics

 1 medium blue solid

 1 medium blue mottled (wing and tail)

 1 pink check

 1 dark pink

 1 medium green

 1 bright yellow

 1 red stripe (plant pot)

 1 plain deep orange-red

ORDER OF APPLIQUÉ

○ Stitch pieces marked A to pieces marked B as described in blocks 1–3.

○ Stitch the appliqué pieces in the order given on the pattern, numbers 1–5.

EMBROIDERY

Hand embroider stamens with stem stitch and French knots. Work the birds' legs in stem stitch, the beaks in satin stitch, and use French knots for the eyes.

ALTERNATIVE USES FOR BLOCK

Minimum block size is 7".

Photocopy at 85% for 6" block.

Photocopy at 170% for a 12" block.

Block 29: *In the Shade*

Block 30 *Big Tulip, Little Birds*

Fabric Requirements

Background fabric

Small scraps of quilting weight cotton fabrics

- 1 dark red
- 1 medium red-orange
- 1 orange print
- 1 dark red (outer layer of heart)
- 1 medium blue
- 1 light blue check
- 1 light green solid
- 1 medium green
- 1 dark green
- 1 bright yellow

ORDER OF APPLIQUÉ

○ Stitch pieces marked A to pieces marked B as described in blocks 1–3.

○ Stitch the heart B to the heart C.

○ Stitch the appliqué pieces in the order given on the pattern, numbers 1–5.

EMBROIDERY

Hand embroider stamens with stem stitch and French knots. Work the birds' beaks in satin stitch and use French knots for the eyes.

ALTERNATIVE USES FOR BLOCK

Minimum block size is 7".
Photocopy at 85% for 6" block.
Photocopy at 170% for a 12" block.

Block 30: *Big Tulip, Little Birds*

Block 31 *The Sculpture*

Fabric Requirements

Background fabric

Main medium red fabric

Main dark red fabric

Small scraps of quilting weight cotton fabrics

    1 red check

    1 medium blue

    1 medium blue dot

    1 large-scale print blue stripe
       (flower pot)

    1 red stripe (tails and wings)

    1 light green

    1 dark green

    1 bright yellow

ORDER OF APPLIQUÉ

○ Stitch pieces marked A to pieces marked B as described in blocks 1–3.

○ Stitch the appliqué pieces in the order given on the pattern, numbers 1–8.

EMBROIDERY

Hand embroider stems from the blue circles to the top of the tulip and the birds' legs in stem stitch. Work the birds' beaks in satin stitch and use French knots for the eyes.

ALTERNATIVE USES FOR BLOCK

Minimum block size is 7". Will fit more comfortably into a 7½" block.

Photocopy at 160% for a 12" block.

Block 31: *The Sculpture*

Block 32 *Love Birds*

Fabric Requirements

Background fabric

Main blue fabric (in tulip)

Main medium red fabric (in tulip)

Small scraps of quilting weight cotton fabrics

  1 dark blue

  1 medium blue (wings)

  1 striped dark blue (tails)

  1 light blue (bodies)

  1 red check

  1 bright yellow

  1 medium green

  1 orange print

ORDER OF APPLIQUÉ

○ Stitch pieces marked A to pieces marked B as described in blocks 1–3.

○ Stitch the appliqué pieces in the order given on the pattern, numbers 1–4. Place the leaves under the stem before the stem is stitched. Do not stitch around the leaves until the blue heart is stitched in place.

EMBROIDERY

Work the birds' beaks in satin stitch and use French knots for the eyes.

ALTERNATIVE USES FOR BLOCK

Minimum block size is 6½". A 7" block will give a more comfortable fit.

Photocopy at 85% for a 6" block.

Photocopy at 170% for a 12" block.

Block 32: *Love Birds*

Block 33 *Patriotic Tulips*

Fabric Requirements

Background fabric

Main blue fabric

Main medium red fabric (wings)

Small scraps of quilting weight cotton fabrics

    1 medium red solid

    1 red & white stripe

    1 yellow multi-dot

    1 medium green

    1 yellow & black

    1 dark blue (tails)

ORDER OF APPLIQUÉ

○ Stitch pieces marked A to pieces marked B as described in blocks 1–3.

○ Stitch the appliqué pieces in the order given on the pattern, numbers 1–6.

EMBROIDERY

Work the birds' beaks in satin stitch, the legs in stem stitch, and use French knots for the eyes.

ALTERNATIVE USES FOR BLOCK

Minimum block size is 6½". A 7" block will give a more comfortable fit.

Photocopy at 85% for a 6" block.

Photocopy at 170% for a 12" block.

Block 33: *Patriotic Tulips*

Block 34 *Tulip Bells*

Fabric Requirements

Background fabric
Main medium red fabric
Main dark red fabric
Small scraps of quilting weight cotton fabrics
    1 medium blue
    1 light blue
    1 medium green
    1 medium pink print
    1 bright yellow

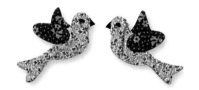

ORDER OF APPLIQUÉ

○ Prepare all appliqué pieces.

○ Stitch green stems to dark red heart.

○ Stitch the birds to the medium red heart.

○ Stitch medium red heart to dark red heart.

○ Stitch the dark red heart to the background fabric.

○ Stitch the remaining parts of the birds to the background fabric. For the tulips, follow the instructions given beside block 13, the Medusa Tulip, page 52.

EMBROIDERY

Hand embroider stamens with stem stitch and French knots. Work the birds' beaks in satin stitch and use French knots for the eyes.

ALTERNATIVE USES FOR BLOCK

Minimum block size is 7".
Photocopy at 85% for a 6" block.
Photocopy at 170% for a 12" block. This pattern fills the whole block and will enlarge well.

Block 34: *Tulip Bells*

Block 35 *Parrot Tulip*

Fabric Requirements

Background fabric

Small scraps of quilting weight cotton fabrics

   1 dark blue

   1 large-scale medium blue print

   1 medium orange-red (heart and ribbon)

   1 medium green multi-dot

   1 dark orange-red (tulip and wings)

   2 different bright yellows

   1 orange print

   1 medium green (small leaves)

Order of Appliqué

   ○ Stitch pieces marked A to pieces marked B as described in blocks 1–3. Stitch the heart B to the heart C.

   ○ Stitch the appliqué pieces in the order given on the pattern, numbers 1–7.

Embroidery

   Hand embroider stamens with stem stitch and French knots. Work the birds' beaks in satin stitch and the legs in stem stitch. Work the eyes in white satin stitch, outlined in black outline stitch. Work a few black satin stitches in the center of the eyes.

Alternative Uses for Block

   Minimum block size is 6½".

   Photocopy at 90% for a 6" block.

   Photocopy at 180% for a 12" block. This pattern fills the whole block and will enlarge well.

Block 35: *Parrot Tulip*

PART 6: *One for the Barn Door*

Hex signs, so popular on barns in Lancaster County, Pennsylvania, can comprise stars, hearts, and tulips. Often circular in shape with a regular geometrical design, this block would translate well into a hex design for a barn door.

Block 36 *The Hex*

Fabric Requirements

Background fabric

Main blue fabric

Small scraps of quilting weight cotton fabrics

    1 dark pink

    1 dark pink & white print

    1 medium green check

    1 orange yellow

    ½ yard of red rickrack braid

ORDER OF APPLIQUÉ

○ Stitch circle A to circle B as described in blocks 1–3. Stitch circle B to circle C.

○ Stitch the appliqué pieces in the order given on the pattern, numbers 1–4.

ALTERNATIVE USES FOR BLOCK

Minimum block size is 7".

Photocopy at 85% for a 6" block.

Photocopy at 170% for a 12" block.

placement line
for braid

3 C
2 B
1 A
X

2

3
2
2
4

Block 36: *The Hex*

PART 7: *The Bonus Blocks*

These two blocks are not in the quilt but each fits well into the tulip and heart theme.

Block 37 *Christmas Tulips*

PHOTO: Alexander Long

Fabric Requirements

Background fabric

Main medium red

Small scraps of quilting weight cotton fabrics

    1 pink-red

    1 green with a red spot

    1 large-scale medium blue

ORDER OF APPLIQUÉ

❍ Stitch the appliqué pieces in the order given on the pattern, numbers 1–4.

ALTERNATIVE USES FOR BLOCK

This block made in bright reds and greens, as illustrated, is a possible choice for a Christmas album quilt.

Minimum block size is 7½".

Photocopy at 160% for a 12" block. Enlargement is recommended.

Pattern can also be set diagonally in a block.

Block 37: *Christmas Tulips*

Block 38 *The Tulip Vase*

PHOTO: Alexander Long

The true Dutch, rather than the Pennsylvania Dutch, take their tulips very seriously. Delft china tulip vases, made especially to hold tulips, come in all shapes, sizes, and prices! Some vases are as tall as a man. The photo shows a modest tulip vase from the author's collection, which is appropriately heart-shaped. This block fits in well with the hearts and tulip theme.

Fabric Requirements

Background fabric

Main medium red fabric

Main dark red fabric

Small scraps of quilting weight cotton fabrics

    1 medium green

    1 yellow stripe

    1 red & white

    1 blue & white large-scale stripe

ORDER OF APPLIQUÉ

○ Stitch pieces marked A to pieces marked B as described in blocks 1–3.

○ Stitch the appliqué pieces in the order given on the pattern, numbers 1–5.

ALTERNATIVE USES FOR BLOCK

Minimum block size is 7½". This is a tight squeeze.

Photocopy at 150% for a 12" block. Enlargement is recommended.

PHOTO: Alexander Long

Block 38: *The Tulip Vase*

PART 8: *Border Appliqué*

Corner blocks

Make 4 corner blocks.

Cutting instructions are on page 20.

This block uses the heart from block 3, large tulips from block 11, and two small tulips from block 20. Use the fabrics as described in blocks 3, 11, and 20.

ORDER OF APPLIQUÉ

○ Stitch pieces marked A to pieces marked B as described in blocks 1–3.

○ Stitch the appliqué pieces in the order given on the pattern, numbers 1–4.

○ Trim to 10¼" x 10¼".

Border strips

Make 4 wide border strips.

Cutting instructions are on page 20.

The patterns for the border strips are in 3 parts. Join the pattern pieces matching the tops and bottoms of each piece. Align the edges of the pattern matching letter A to A and B to B; C indicates the end of the border strip where it joins the corner block.

The appliqué design uses tulips from blocks 11, 17, 20, and 27. Use the same fabrics for the border tulips as were used in the blocks.

ORDER OF APPLIQUÉ

○ Stitch pieces marked A to pieces marked B as described in blocks 1–3.

○ Stitch the appliqué pieces in the order given on the pattern, numbers 1–9.

○ Add the red half circles (see detailed instructions, page 21).

○ Trim to 10¼" wide.

○ Add the red half circles to the 4 narrow outer borders (see detailed instructions, page 24).

○ Trim to 2" wide.

○ Continue with the quilt assembly as described in Chapter 2.

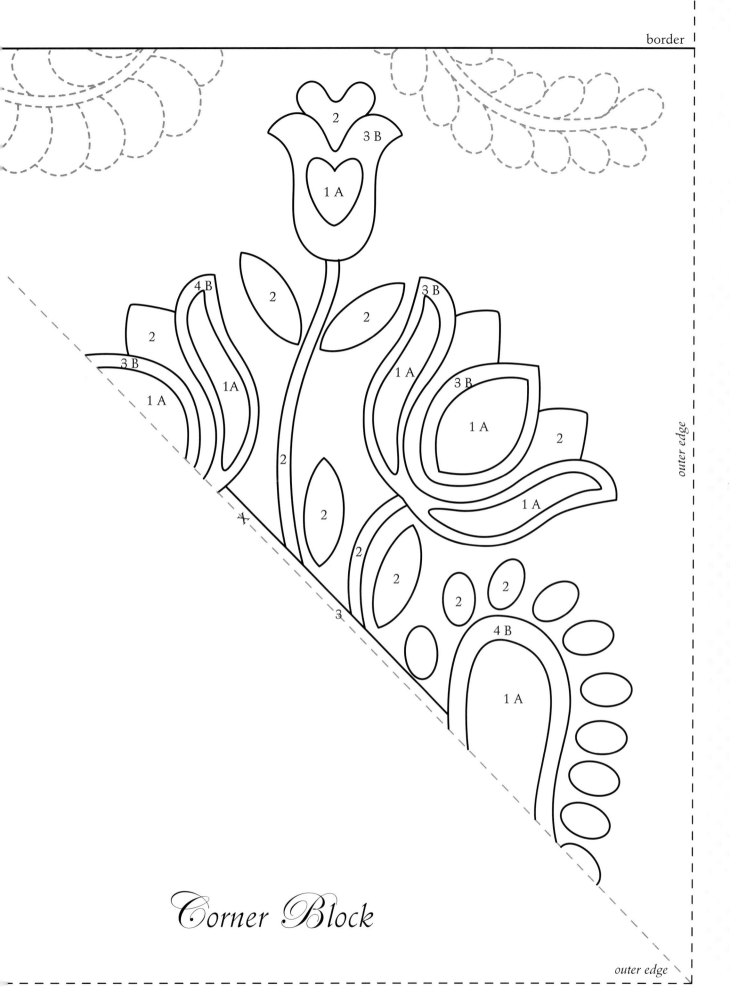

outer edge

2

3 B

1 A

4 B

2

2

3 B

3 B

1 A

1 A

1 A

3 B

1 A

2

2

2

2

2

2

4

3

2

2

2

1 A

4 B

1 A

Corner Block

outer edge

center of border

to end of border strip

A

2

1 A 4 B

1 A

4 B

3

2

4

1 A

5 B

2

2

3

2

2

2

1 A

5 B

4

2

3 B

1 A

2

2

5

2

1 A

3 B

4

1 A

6

Border Strip

Hearts & Tulips ⚘ Margaret Docherty

A

A   B

to end of border strip

2 B
1 A
3 B
1 A
4 B
1 A
1 A
2 B
1 A
1 A
5 B
1 A

2

1 A
5 B
1 A 2 B
1 A
1 A
3 B
1 A
4 B
2
1 A
3 B
1 A
2 B
2

2

2

2
2

5
3
9
4
6
1 A
7
8 B
2

top of
half circle trim

A   B

A

B

to end of border strip

3 B

2 B

1 A

2

1 A

5 B

2

5 B

1 A

5 B

2

4

5 B

1 A

4

2

5 B

1 A

4

Border Strip

A

B

Hearts & Tulips ❧ Margaret Docherty

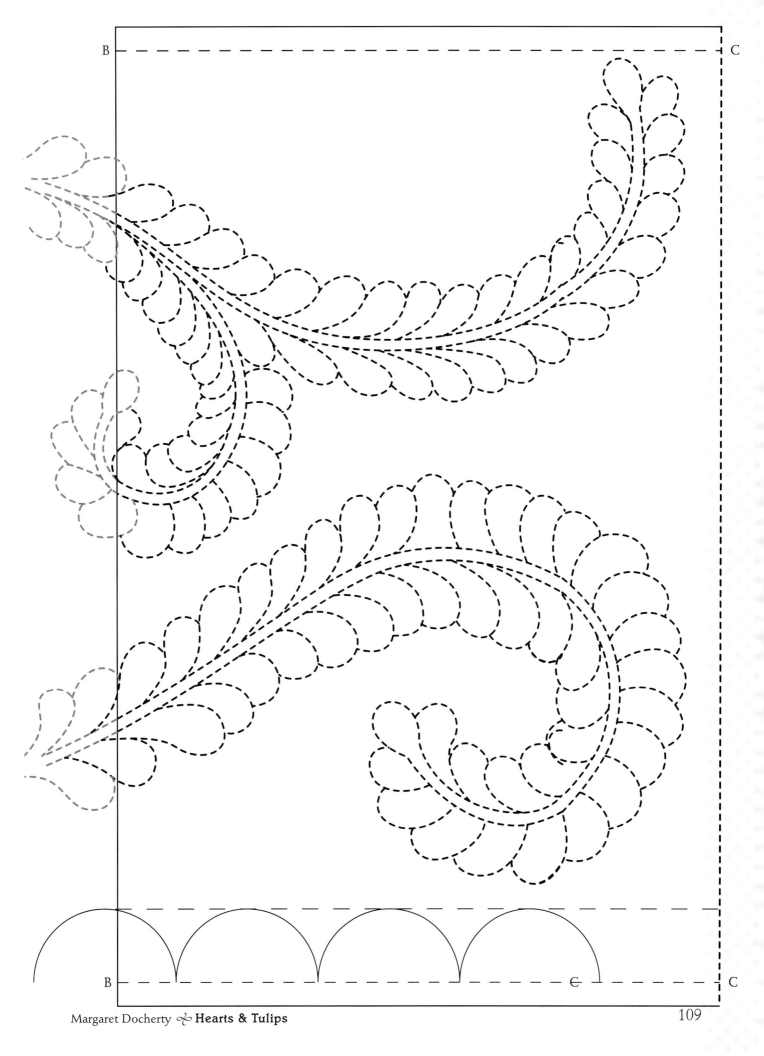

Bibliography

Docherty. Margaret. *Appliqué Masterpiece: Little Brown Bird Patterns.*
Paducah, KY: American Quilter's Society, 2000.

Ferrier, Beth. *Hand Appliqué by Machine,* Saginaw, MI: Applewood
Farm Publications, 2006.

Gaudynski, Diane. *Quilt Savvy: Gaudynski's Machine Quilting Guidebook.*
Paducah, KY: American Quilter's Society, 2002.

Hargrave, Harriet. *Heirloom Machine Quilting, 4th Edition: Comprehensive
Guide to Hand-Quilting Effects Using Your Sewing Machine.*
Lafayette, CA: C&T Publishing, Inc., 2004.

_____. *Mastering Machine Appliqué: The Complete Guide Including Invisible
Machine Appliqué, Satin Stitch, Blanket Stitch and Much More.* Lafayette,
CA: C&T Publishing, Inc., 2001.

Nickels, Sue. *Machine Appliqué, A Sampler of Techniques.* Paducah, KY:
American Quilter's Society, 2001.

_____. *Machine Quilting, A Primer of Techniques.* Paducah, KY:
American Quilter's Society, 2003.

Olson, Claudia. *Two-Block Appliqué Quilts.* Woodinville, WA:
Martingale & Company, 2004.

Meet the Author

PHOTO: Huw Evans

Margaret, like most 21st-century women, combines a "proper" job with running a house, a family, a garden, and pets. She thinks that every woman needs to escape the daily drudgery from time to time and should have a hobby. Hers is sewing.

Always considered handy with a needle or sewing machine, Margaret ceased to be useful when she discovered quilting over 20 years ago. Not long after, she learned that houses, gardens, and families could run themselves quite adequately and leave more time for quilting. The day job, as a pediatrician, continues. It acts as a distraction from the unending grind of stitching fabric.

Her advice to all potential quilters is to get a good husband and keep him. Margaret is still married to her original husband, or at least he looks uncannily like him. Early on in your marriage, introduce your husband to the joys of cooking and shopping. You will reap rewards in later years when he is devoted to his kitchen and you can dedicate your time to "finishing that quilt."